The Fire Waits

The Fire Waits

**Prayers and Poems
for the Sabbath and Festivals**

Michael T. Hecht

HARTMORE HOUSE
Bridgeport, Connecticut

TO THE MEMORY OF
ANNA VALENSTEIN

PREFACE

Each generation has its own special concerns. In the past, Jewish poets supplemented the "official" prayers of the synagogue with their own creations, expressing the hopes and fears of their day.

The invention of printing, along with other factors, tended to freeze the living tradition, so that today's prayerbooks are largely similar and contain very little modern poetic expression. Thus, there are Jews who pray regularly for the welfare of the ancient scholars of Babylonia, but who make no reference in their worship to the Holocaust, the rebirth of Israel, or other aspects of life in our own era.

On the other hand, some Jews have rather freely changed the prayerbook. But some of their prayers, which seemed so current when composed, became dated soon after publication.

Faced with such alternatives, many religious leaders have been providing their congregations with supplementary prayers, contemporary prayer booklets, or even complete services—all of which are meant to be used for a time and then replaced. (A High Holiday prayer book has even been printed with loose-leaf pages!)

The prayers and poems in this volume were originally created for congregational use. Most of them take as their starting point a verse from the weekly Torah portion or from one of the traditional commentaries on such a text.

This collection includes a prayer, poem, or meditation for each week of the year. The Hebrew name of the weekly Biblical portion and the verse references are provided. It is suggested that the reader consult the original verses.

Prayers for special Sabbaths and for the holidays have also been included.

I am grateful to Mr. and Mrs. Morris Speizman, of Charlotte, North Carolina, who so actively encouraged the publication of these pages.

The Torah was my inspiration. My intention was to fulfill the imperative, "Turn it and turn it, for everything is in it."

MICHAEL HECHT

Cleveland Heights, Ohio
May 1972

TABLE OF CONTENTS

HOLY DAYS AND SPECIAL SABBATHS 122

The Fire Waits

WHY DO YOU NEED US?

"God created man in His image . . . .
And God blessed them . . . .
And God saw all that He had made
And it was very good."

>But man saw all that God had made,
>Especially himself,
>And could not be persuaded it was good.

Wise men debated, wise men concluded:
Better for man
Had he never been created.
(But now that he has been created
Let him consider well his deeds.)

>God, why do You need us?
>To what purpose all this birth and dying?
>What was wrong with the perfection of darkness
>And the splendor of nothing?

Or we could understand Your joy
In billions of suns
Gliding through limitless spaces
With mathematical certainty.

>But what joy in us?
>Sometimes we praise You, more often revile You.
>Sometimes we delight in Your creation.
>Too often we destroy it.

The mouse gnawing at the lion's bonds
Once showed the lion that a mouse can be of service.
What is our service to You?

> The answer lies dimly in our hearts:
> We are more than we seem.
> We have the power to shake earth's foundations
> With our acts of creativity.
> You have made us co-creators of the world.

Like Your creation, ours must be not merely
That of mathematical certainties,
But of ourselves.

> We are not finished products.
> We are still becoming. We are potential men.
> You have set us to the molding of ourselves.

Let it be said:
Man saw all that God had made,
Especially himself,
And saw that it could be good.
Man saw that God needed him to make man.

> May we come to serve Your purpose.
> "May the glory of the Lord be forever;
> May the Lord rejoice in His works!"

Genesis 1. Eruvin 13b. Psalms 104

BUT IF THAT CANNOT BE

God, can You still put up with man?
Can You bear his deeds?

> "The Lord saw that man's wickedness on earth was great
> And that the bent of all his thoughts was
> Only evil all the time,
> So that the Lord was sorry for making man on earth,
> And His heart was saddened."

Is Your heart not saddened now?
Can You stand the cries of starving children?
Can You bear the screams of prisoners?

> "The Lord thought,
> 'I will erase from the face of the earth
> Mankind which I have created.' "

And yet perhaps we can be saved
The way it happened once before:

> "But Noah found favor in the sight of the Lord."

One man! For one man You preserved life.
Give us the strength to be the sort of men and women
For whom the world should be saved:

> "Noah was a good man, blameless in his age;
> Noah walked with God."

Noah did not rise to change an evil world—
Greater men than Noah were to come—
And yet it was enough he walked with God.

> If only we could feel the hurt of all our fellow men!
> But if that cannot be, then let us be like Noah.
> If we cannot save the world,
> Then let us prove the world worth saving.

It is enough if we be good people—
And, God, it is not easy.
When all men cheat, it is hard not to cheat.
When all men lie, it is hard not to lie.

> So few are the heroes of our age!
> So many bend to every evil wind!

If only we could change the world!
But if that cannot be, then let us be like Noah.
Let us be worth saving.

> Where there are no heroes,
> Let us be heroes of a sort.
> May we be blameless in our age.
> May we walk with God.

Genesis 6:5–9 Rashi

CHILDLESS

"The word of the Lord came to Abram in a vision:
'Do not fear, Abram, I am you shield.
Your reward shall be very great.'

    "But Abram said, 'Lord God, what can You give me
    While I go childless!' "

Abraham had everything; but he had nothing.
Without posterity he felt as a dead man.

    It is common to have children.
    Each of us was someone's child.

Children are born in our pain.
And if, with pain, we raise them,
We do not know what we have done.

    They look like us. They talk like us.
    They walk like us—even as we bear the imprint
    Of those who went before us.

But they are not ourselves, we learn in pain.
And many blessed with sons and daughters
Yet have said:
Lord God, what can You give me,
For I am childless!

    It happened to Abraham, who cried out,
    "Oh that Ishmael might live in Your presence!"
    Ishmael lived, but not in Your presence,
    "His hand against everyone,
    And everyone's hand against him."
    He was Abraham's son, but he was not Abraham's
       posterity.

19

Isaac was Abraham's son,
And Jacob was Isaac's son—
And we are the sons of Abraham, of whom You said,
"Israel my servant,
Jacob whom I have chosen,
The seed of Abraham who loved Me."

> Where did Abraham go wrong with Ishmael?
> And what did Abraham do right for Isaac?
> Why are we, the sons of Abraham, so few?
> What can we do to have sons like Isaac?
> What can You give us, Lord,
> So that we shall not be childless?

We ask the question in our anguish.
Let us not have pain for nothing,
Nor have children for confusion.
May they be the seed of those blessed of the Lord
And their posterity with them.

> Help us be the sort of people
> Whose children will want
> To be our posterity.

Genesis 15:1; 16:12; 17:18. Isaiah 41:8; 65:23

YOUR PEOPLE PROTESTS

"Will You really destroy the good with the wicked? . . .
Far be it from You!
Shall the Judge of all the earth not do justice?"

> Abraham teaching You, God, to be just.
> You were right that time.
> There was no decent man in all of Sodom.
> Sodom deserved its flaming death.

But what would Abraham say today?

> Many wealthy, happy men are living now
> Who could have taught the Sodomites a trick or two,
> While a million Jewish children
> Are cinders in the wind.

Does the Judge of all the earth not do justice!

> We are the children of Abraham.
> We cannot accept the cruelty of life.
> We cannot humbly say, "God's will be done."
> This cannot be God's will!

Your people still protests:
Cruelty and hate,
Pain and starvation
Are not the things we would allow
If we were Master of the world.

> We cannot bow to the inevitable.
> We do not accept the verdict of history!

In memory of Abraham,
In memory of the good men of all time,
In the name of those million children—

> In reverence of Your name,
> That it be not tarnished—
> We will fight.

In Israel we take our stand
And cry: Enough!
This is the place for justice
For us and for our children!

> And still children die
> While smiling men of Sodom have their way.
> But we shall not accept it
> Here or anywhere.

Again Your children rise to challenge You:
Shall the Judge of all the earth not do justice!

> You would not have it any other way.
> Abraham was Your delight.
> Help us be like him.
> Help us help You create the world.

Genesis 18:23–25

22

OLD SIGHTS, YOUNG EYES

The Torah tells what Abraham did when Sarah died;
It does not tell us how he felt.

> He mourned his wife and bought a place of burial,
> Then set his thoughts upon the future
> And found for his son a worthy wife.

Abraham's emotions are not told in holy writ.
Those who have endured a loss like Abraham's
Do not need to be informed—

> While those who have been spared
> Would little comprehend a tale of twenty pages.

Isaac loved Rebeccah—that the Torah tells.
But what that means can never be explained.
Only those who have known love understand how Isaac
    felt.

> Each generation must learn everything itself!

No one understands his parents till he is a parent.
Only the victims comprehend the agony of war.
Joy and sorrow are but words to those who have not felt
    them,
Just as the rainbow is the blind man's mystery.

> This is man's sorrow:
> That each of us must touch entrancing flames
> To learn in pain the power of fire.

This, too, is man's glory.
For if we knew what those before us felt
Then we would not be ourselves. We would be they.

We would go through the motions of life,
But life would belong to those who felt it first.

And if our children knew the answers
Before life asked the questions,
Man would have no history.

We thank You, God, that when we see old sights
We see them fresh and not through others' eyes.

Thank You, God, that each of us is a new world,
That each of us finds by himself the joys of life,
That each of us, through sorrow, can by himself find You.

Thank You for the fresh experiences of each new
day.

Genesis 23; 24:67

24

BROTHERS

"Esau hated Jacob
For the blessing which his father gave him."

> For Hottentots and other distant folk
> Our hearts are filled with noble love.
> It is only people whom we know that we dislike.
> And if they are so close to us
> That we are tied by bonds of love,
> Then there is room for greater hate.

"Esau hated Jacob
For the blessing which his father gave him;
And Esau thought, 'Soon my father will be dead,
And I will kill Jacob my brother.' "

> "Jacob my brother"! Seeing no irony.
> "For the blessing"!
> Why must blessings bring such curses?

Why is a mother's love a source of pain;
A father's pride, a cause of bitterness?
Many a man who would rebuild the world
On deep foundations of eternal love
Cannot bear the sight of his own brother.

> The Hottentots we never meet.
> It is family and friends who fill our life.
> And if we care to make a better world,
> We ought to start by loving them.

The city so beautiful when sighted from the air
Is smoke and dust and shacks and garbage cans
For us who walk its streets.
Far greater is the artist who sees beauty
In its ugliness
Than one who paints the view without the people.

> Teach us, God, to love what is close to home—
> Our brothers, our companions, those who work with
>   us,
> The people that we see, the streets we walk,
> The crowds we jostle as we seek our daily bread.
> You do not regard our love for Hottentots.
> Man's record in Your book is that of Jacob and his
>   Esau.

"Jacob my brother." Yes, my brother.
Help us say the word with joy.
We have more brothers every day,
Competitors who gasp at air that we would breathe,
Who envy us our blessings, as we envy theirs.

> The world of love we would create
> Dies daily in ourselves,
> Though in our souls alone it can find birth.

This is our prayer, God of love:
Help us to love
Those we have to love.

Genesis 27:41

THE GATE OF HEAVEN

"Jacob woke and said,
'Indeed the Lord is in this place, though I did not know it.'
He trembled and said, 'How awesome is this place!
This is none other than the house of God,
And this is the gate of heaven!'"

    The gate of heaven! How we envy Jacob's vision!
    Our own nights pass unblessed by visions of eternity.

Jacob was a lonely wanderer, full of fear.
What he glimpsed that night transformed him.
We are lonely wanderers.
Where is the vision that You have for us?

    The mystics of the East sought entrance to Your
       house.
    Intoxicating music, dizzying dances, strong drugs,
    The flagellation of their own bare backs
    Removed them from their cares for but a while.
    For an hour they ceased being flesh and blood,
    But then they fell and could not bear their loss of
       vision.

Men often try to rise above this world of drudgery and tears.
Opiates vie with self-inflicted visions of a better day.
Mobs march with banners,
Their eyes, reflecting torchlight, focused on another world.

    The mobs grow old.
    Middle-aged former marchers have lustreless eyes.
    Where is the gate of heaven?

27

Jacob was the gate of heaven.
Jacob's vision was not one of You, but of himself.
In his dream he saw that there was meaning
In his wandering and his strife.

> Jacob did not reach Your realm.
> He saw only that Your realm is real.
> He could believe in life.

He could believe that guarding sheep was serving You.
He could believe that raising children was a way of finding
  You.
He could believe that living in this ordinary world
Was the way to reach for worlds unknown.

> Grant us the same vision, Lord.
> Let us see that there is meaning in our everyday.
> Then our eyes will never dim.
> Help us see—we are the gate of heaven.

Genesis 28:16–17

THE WAY HOME

On Jacob's journey home he had to meet his brother—
Esau, whom he had cheated; Esau, who had sworn to kill him;
Esau, on the journey home.

> Each of the brothers thought of the past—
> One, of wrongs he had committed,
> The other, of injustice done to him;
> One, of exile suffered for his sins,
> The other, of tears of anguish he had shed.

The brothers came for battle, as brothers often do,
But Jacob pleaded for forgiveness.
Before he met his brother, he sent offerings—
Goats and sheep, camels, cows, and asses—
And a message:
"These belong to your slave Jacob.
They are an offering sent to my lord Esau."

> Jacob thought, "Maybe he will forgive me."
> "Jacob bowed seven times before he reached his
>   brother.
> Then Esau ran to meet him, hugged him,
> Fell on his neck and kissed him.
> They wept."

Reconciliation. Forgiveness. An end to useless quarrels.
Two brothers buried hate
Because one was humble enough to say, I am sorry;
And the other, forgiving enough not to mention former sins.

> Esau is always on the journey home.
> Every man must meet the many brothers he has
>   wronged.
> Each of us is Jacob. Each of us is Esau.
> Each of us is questing for his home—
> The person that he ought to be.

When it is our turn to be like Jacob,
God, help us to admit our wrongs. Help us to be humble.
Strengthen us to seek forgiveness from our brothers.
Let us not perish in our pride,
Nor suffocate in self-justification.

> When it is our turn to be like Esau,
> God, let us be forgiving. Help us to forget the past.
> Help us to erase from our eyes
> Bitter memories that blind us.
> Help us to meet our brothers.
> Help us to find the way home.

Genesis 32–33

30

HOMICIDE REPORT

"Do you recognize this, Jacob? It's a coat. We found it.
Those are blood spots . . . . Are you sure it's his—Joseph's?
I'm sorry, sir, deeply sorry . . . .
Of course, we'll do our best. I'm sure we'll find him . . . ."

> Was there a policeman in those days to give the news
>   to Jacob?
> And did the man go home and say, "It's been a rough
>   day, honey"?
> Taking off his shoes, did he mutter,
> "Poor guy . . . . I'm glad it wasn't my boy.
> I hope I'm not there when they find what's left"?

Next day, dictating the report:
"File under *Homicides, Suspected: Wild Beasts*.
The deceased—Hebrew—age 17. Remains not found.
That makes three this year. Case closed."

> The neighbors came to Jacob.
> What could they say?
> They sat in silence broken only by
> Jacob's cries.

No use. Jacob would not be consoled.
The neighbors were ashamed they could not help.
They blamed Jacob. They blamed themselves.

> Perhaps they never realized
> How much they were doing
> In reaching out to Jacob;
> But they felt it.

31

In suffering with Jacob
They affirmed themselves.
They ennobled suffering.

> In offering Jacob their presence and their tears
> They said: You matter, Jacob—we all matter very much.

Death has visited you, Jacob.
It will come to us.

> We should get used to it. We don't.
> Your tragedy is also ours.

At the police station your son has become
Homicides, Suspected: Wild Beasts: File 3.
But for us there is a memory. He was a person.

* * *

> God, we thank You
> For letting us feel our neighbor's loss,
> For letting his tragedy wound us.

These are wounds that heal us, wounds of love.
From them we understand that when we, too, shall die,
Our passing will be felt.

> In giving sympathy to others
> We hear Your voice.
> You say: Man, My creature, you matter to Me.

Genesis 37:29—35

NIGHTMARES

Tremble, Egypt!
Pharaoh has had nightmares.
The wise men are conferring.
What can be the meaning of the dreams?

> Seven fat cows; seven lean.
> Seven fine ears; seven mean.
> Lean and mean eat fat and fine.
> This must surely be a sign!

What will tomorrow bring?
War? Pestilence? Famine?
We are afraid.

> The future is unknown.
> Tomorrow is concealed.
> Let us fear it.

Only Joseph knows the answer:
"Pharaoh, do not fear the future.
I have had my dreams, like you.
Yours is not a nightmare, if you will not have it so.
God has given you the power to thwart nightmares.

> "Make the future happen.
> Do not succumb to your bad dreams.
> That is God's message to Pharaoh."

Humble people have their nightmares, too,
Sleeping or awake.
There are those who cannot sleep
For waking dreams of horror.

      We, too, are afraid.
      Help us, God. Remove our nightmares!
Health is a gift we fear You may take back.
Prosperity can vanish in a day.
We fear for our children.
We fear for our lives.
We fear fear.

      Take away these nightmares, God!
      Why have we deserved them?
      Or, strengthen us against them.
      Let them not rule us.

Put our dreams into our hands.
Help us make our nightmares false.

      Save us from inaction.
      Let us be the masters of our dreams.

Genesis 41

BLINDNESS

When Benjamin went down to Egypt
These were his sons:
Bela, Becher, Ashbel, Gera, Naaman, Ehi, Rosh,
Muppim and Huppim, and Ard.

> We always think of Benjamin
> As just a little boy,
> Jacob's baby.

If today he had a birthday
We. would likely send a gift
For a four-year old.

> He grew,
> And we never knew.

If we were Benjamin,
We surely would resent it.

> But every day
> Mothers look at grown sons
> And see babies.

Every day men look at other men
And see only doctors, lawyers, or butchers—
Not men.

> Every day
> Men behind cannons
> Do not see other men at all—
> Only The Enemy.

What is wrong with our sight?
God, what is this blindness?
Why can we not see others
As they see themselves?

> All we seem to notice
> Is what we want to see,
> Not what we need to see.

We are blind, God!
Where is the cure?

> We seek the cure for many illnesses.
> Give us the desire to find remedy also for this.
> For this blindness brings death.

Help us find life.
Open our eyes to our fellow men.

Genesis 46:21

VAYEHI

LORD, I HOPE

A life of turmoil is about to end.
Jacob is dying.
Is he incoherent when he cries,
"Lord, I hope for your salvation"?

> What does he mean? What can be his message?

Living, I have hoped.
Dying, I still hope.
Looking to the future of my sons,
I have great hope.

> You, my children, also have your times of hoping.
> When your wives are in the pangs of birth
> You raise your eyes in prayer to God.

But that is nothing, children.
What will you do when hopes are dashed?
What will you do if God does not answer?
What will you do?

> Will you still hope?
> You must.

What will you do when all you work for fails?
What will you do when others turn away from you—
When your friends shun you?
What will you do when your own flesh turns from you?

> Will you still have hope?
> You must.

37

What will you do when you are old? . . .
The doctor says, "The machine is wearing out."
The young people say,
"You just don't—can't—understand."

> Lord, I hope for Your salvation,
> Even as my life is fading.

Men are worse than devils.
If there are devils, we can trust them to be evil.
Men are confusing.
We have to trust them—we are men.

> Trust in mankind
> Even though men burn your flesh.
> Like me, in your last hour,
> Have hope for your seed.

> What shall I give to you, my sons?
> This is my treasure—
> Hope.

Genesis 49: 18 Midrash Rabbah

HEAVY MOUTHS, SLOW TONGUES

Moses, when You called him, cried,
"I am not a man of words . . .
My mouth is heavy; and my tongue is slow."

> You call us, too;
> And who are we to speak for You?

We rarely find the words to tell our love—
And if we do, we say so many other things
That wound and hurt, that no one hears our loving words.

> And all the things we should have said
> Rise up to haunt us on that day
> When nothing can be said
> To one who can no longer hear.

And who are we to be Your spokesmen
To our children?
Speech is an art we have not learned.
Sometimes we shout—and we are saying nothing.

> On the street we meet a friend
> Proudly wearing a brand-new hat.
> We mean to notice it and cause some little joy,
> But in our haste we do not speak.

Over coffee, over cards,
When we sit and when we walk,
Early in the morning, late at night,
We speak to neighbors about neighbors.

> Do we realize what we say?
> Sometimes we are ashamed.

We are your spokesmen, God,
For You have let us do Your work.
Your voice is heard through ours.
Help us do Your will!

> We thank You for moments of understanding
> That make this world go on.
> We thank You for words that heal,
> Words that instruct,
> Words that others take into their hearts.

We have spoken such words, too—
But not as often as we would.

> Do for us what You promised Moses:
> "I will be with you when you speak."
> Help us to speak with love and skill.
> Let us be Your messengers in truth.

Exodus 4:10–11

A RACE OF GODS

"All the water in the Nile turned to blood,
And all the fish in the Nile died,
And the Nile stank . . . .
But since the magicians of Egypt could do the same
By their science,
Pharaoh took courage and did not listen . . . ."

     Pharaoh was complacent:
     I, too, am a god.
     My science gives me power.
     How can the God of the Hebrews impress me?

If Pharoah was a god,
Then we are a race of gods.

     Could he turn his rivers into blood?
     We can make ours into sewage.

On the banks of the Nile
Monuments still stand
To Pharaoh's glory.

     Tourists come by day to marvel.
     Jackals come by night to laugh.
     The monuments remain.
     The people are dead. Pharaoh is dead.

Pharaoh never thought of people.
They were there to serve technology.
Hebrew slaves? Fine workers when left alone.
If only Moses and Aaron would not agitate.
Who do they think they are?

> When Pharaoh grew too proud, You swore:
> "Against all the gods of Egypt
> I will wreak judgments."

Are You wreaking judgments against us,
Letting us create water we cannot drink,
Air we cannot breathe,
Bacteria we cannot kill,
Cities we cannot live in?

> Are these Your plagues on us
> For being so taken with our own power?

Exodus 7:20–22; 12:12

OUR LIGHT

The ninth plague:
"Moses stretched his hand out toward the sky,
And there came thick darkness over the land of Egypt . . .
Men could not see their brothers . . . .

"But the people of Israel had light in their homes."

Egypt's darkness was darkness of the soul.
Men could not see their brothers.
No justice for the stranger; no pity for the slave.

The Israelites had light—in their homes.
Was it not Moses' own mother who taught him to
see?

"When Moses had grown
He went out to his brothers
And saw their sufferings.
And he saw an Egyptian striking a Hebrew,
One of his brothers."

Moses, the Egyptian prince, saw
What others could not see,
Because the people of Israel had light
In their homes.

We still see by that light.
The Sabbath candles say:
"Your male and female servant shall rest, like you.
Remember that you were a slave in the land of Egypt."

    Near the Sabbath lights stands the little box—
    It jingles when you lift it:
    Kindle the lights after remembering the poor.

The Yahrzeit light says:
"May He bring His kingdom in your lifetime."
They have not died who worked for that kingdom.
Their lives are not forgotten.
We still see them.
We remember how they saw their brothers.

    How shall we see by that light
    If we do not remember our brothers
    And think of their sufferings?

Exodus 10:22–23; 2:11. Kaddish

FORGOTTEN MIRACLES

"Is the Lord in our midst or not?"
How could Your people doubt,
When they themselves had seen
The wall of water sweep away the chariots of Pharaoh?

> How could they doubt You,
> Getting water from a rock,
> Manna from the sky?

How could they keep forgetting
Your daily miracles?

> How can we see children born
> And watch them grow,
> And not know we have seen miracles?

How can we be saved from death
By preparations made from moldy brews
And doubt Your miracles?

> How can we see the beauty that surrounds us—
> Made by God or fashioned by man—
> And not thank You?

How can we see men doing acts of kindness,
When it is easier to be cruel,
And not exclaim: A miracle!

> We who sit by the fleshpots
> And eat our fill of bread
> Are much more ready to curse You for evil
> Than to bless You for good.

Do we ever ask by what great right
We, of all Your creatures that have ever lived,
Should enjoy riches and health
Of which Pharaoh never dreamt.

> Why do we presume You owe us life and health and
>   peace?
> You owe us nothing, God,
> And everything that You provide is a new miracle.

Even a moment of life, each breath,
Each thing we see,
Everything we feel,
Is a miracle.

> We have hearts that fear
> And minds that doubt,
> We can think the thought,
> "Is the Lord in our midst?"–
> All this is a miracle.

We are a miracle.
How can You not be in our midst?

Exodus 17:7

WE DID NOT CHOOSE

We did not choose the greatness
That You ask of us.

> We would have slunk back to Egypt,
> If only You had let Your people go.

You stood us at a smoking mountain,
Making us give assent to being
What we did not want to be:
A kingdom of priests and a holy people.

> Why us? Why anyone?
> Why did You make us swear not to swear falsely.
> We wanted to be—and we have been—false.
> We have served other gods,
> Gods that gave us
> No undeserved, unwanted honors.

Our ancestors were slaves
And gladly would have remained slaves.

> Slaves have no honor
> And no morals.
> Slaves take no oaths
> And do not have to keep their word.
> Slaves are the freest of men.

Why priests? Why holy?
Why must we always feel Your disappointment.

> We cannot escape You.
> The world does not forget our dignity
> Even if it has to make it our shame.

Sometimes we are not priests,
But sacrificial lambs whose blood is shed
To make atonement to an enraged world
That wishes it had never heard
Your awesome word.

So have kings thought when weary.
They abdicated their honor.
They thought they could be commoners.
They became, not commoners, but former kings.

You give us not much choice.
Either we are priests—or we are degraded priests.
You will not let us turn to slaves again.

We can be what we must be with joy;
Or we can refuse
And know always
We have turned our back on greatness.

Help us to accept our destiny with joy.
We could not slink back to Egypt then.
We cannot do it now.
Always we stand at Mount Sinai.

Let us answer when You ask for our assent:
We will obey.

Exodus 19:6

YOU WILL NOT LET US REST

"These are the laws which you shall set before them."
God to Moses; Moses to us—
The laws have been transmitted, read, studied.
But we are still the same.

> Read laws to the sea—
> And the tides will still roll
> By the dictates of the moon.

Read laws to an ant—
And it will not pause for an instant
In its frantic search for food.

> Read laws to man. Can he obey them?
> Or is he chained, like the sea, like the ant,
> To what he has been and must be?

We understand Your laws.

> Murder brings murder.
> Deceit brings deceit.
> Oppression brings oppression.
> Curses bring curses.

Kindness brings kindness.
Truth brings truth.
Freedom brings freedom.
Blessings bring blessings.

> We know.
> We have read the laws.

They puzzle us.
Because although we know
That they are right—
We cannot keep them. Too often
We obey instinct, and not laws;
We obey nature, and not God.

> Murder, deceit, oppression, and curses
> Are our lot as much as
> Kindness, truth, freedom, and blessings.

And still You will not let us rest,
But read us laws.

> This makes us human,
> Not like the sea, nor like the ant.
> We live in two realms:
> The realm of *is*
> And the realm of *ought*.

We must always be uneasy,
Elated by the challenge that You give us,
Dissatisfied with what we do each day.

> Read us the laws.
> If we can keep but one of them,
> It is worthwhile.

Exodus 21:1

TOO MUCH POWER

"Let them make for Me a sanctuary,
That I may dwell in their midst."

> God, You must be our tenant—
> Though the universe is Yours,
> And You are Lord of all the earth.

Unless we let You in,
Unless we make a place for You,
You cannot dwell with us.

> You give us too much power:
> You let us rule the creatures of the earth and sea—
> And we exploit them and destroy.

You make us masters of our history—
It is a tale of suffering and blood.

> You give us control over Your very presence—
> And we have shut You out.

What are the opposites of sanctuaries?
Those we have built—palaces of lies,
Walls that keep Your presence out.

> Can You enter our homes, our schools, our theatres,
> And find a place to rest?

Do You not feel a stranger
Even where we mention Your name
While our thoughts stray far from You?

> We do not want to destroy.
> We do not want to write our history in flame and
>   blood.
> We do not want to shut You out.
> We cannot help ourselves.

Something makes us use our power to destroy.
We are not wise enough for wisdom.

> "Let them make for Me a sanctuary,
> That I may dwell in their midst."

That is what we want to do!
We know: Without You we are as the dead.
We are soon gone, nor has the race of man eternal life.
Our power has no power.

> Help us find true wisdom—
> Or You must take away our power to deny You.
> Reveal Yourself again to us.

Exodus 25:8

52

FLAME BEGETS FLAME

"Let them bring you clear olive oil . . .
To cause a lamp to burn always . . .
Before the Lord . . . ."

> A lamp that kindles other lamps
> Is not diminished—

And if that lamp grows cold,
The flame it shared
Can be returned
To kindle it again.

> Flame begets flame;
> Hearts kindle hearts,
> So that the sacred fire
> Never dies.

Where are the hearts
Whose light can kindle ours?

> Where are our fathers
> Whose hearts' glow
> Lit flames of faith
> Through centuries of night?

Where are our children
To rekindle our flame—

> Not from the altars of other gods,
> But from the Eternal Light
> Of Your presence?

Where are we?
Where are our flaming hearts
To kindle others?

> We live in shadows:
> Indecision, fear,
> Weakness of spirit.

Where yet there is a flame,
However weak,
Help us, God, to keep that fire alive.
Help us fan it with Your breath.

> Help us pass the flame to others.
> One heart's flame is all we ask—
> Our own.

Exodus 27:20–21

A STATUE OF OURSELVES

"When the people saw that Moses was slow
In coming down from the mountain,
Then the people pressed against Aaron and said to him:
'Get up and make us a god to walk before us,
Since What's-his-name . . . Moses . . .
The man who brought us out of the land of Egypt . . .
We do not know what has become of him.' "

> Moses was not dead then;
> But now all the great men are gone
> Who had it in their power
> To make us worship You.

You understand, God:
We are weak . . .
And You are so abstract . . .

> Somehow we cannot live without a god;
> And if, without Moses, we cannot find You,
> Then some other god will have to do.

Just recently
We were doing very well.
We found a god
Much better than a golden calf.

> Man became his own god.
> We ourselves were god.

We did not need You any more.
The books all said so.
We learned it in school.

> We believed in Man, who could bestow
> Enlightenment,
> Brotherhood,
> Peace and Plenty.

We danced about a statue of ourselves,
But Man's promises have not come true.

> So Man is joining forgotten gods,
> And we must go about again
> Looking for a god to walk before us.

God, walk in our midst,
Even though we are as stiff-necked as our fathers.
Forgive our sin and our error,
And make us Yours.

> We still need You, God.

Exodus 32:1; 34:9

THE WHOLE COMMUNITY

"Moses called together the whole community of the
Israelites . . . . 'Take from among you an offering to the
Lord . . . gold, silver, and copper . . . .' After the whole
community of the Israelites left Moses' presence . . . they
brought the Lord's offering for the construction of the
Tent of Meeting . . . ."

> The whole community!
> United,
> Willing to hear God's word,
> Anxious to erect His Sanctuary.

Such unity was not to be attained again
In times of peace.

> When David faced the Philistines
> Again there was unity.

When the ghetto walls closed in
There had to be unity.

> When Hitler searched for Jews
> We all became brothers.

During the Miracles of June
We were as one.

> But not in times of peace.

Lord, give us understanding.
Let us see that
Every time is one of war.

> There is always danger.
> There is always fear.

Hatred is as natural to earth as air;
Jealousy and greed, as much a part of man
As two eyes, ten fingers, or his clever brain.

> And these eyes, these fingers, this brain
> Excel in making instruments of evil.

What is history if not
A list of dead men
And the boasts of generals
That they best oversaw destruction?

> There is no peace—
> And we must be united now.

We must be brothers against hatred
Or die.

> God, may we live to be
> The whole community,
> United,
> Willing to hear God's word,
> Anxious to erect Your Sanctuary.

Exodus 35

HOLY TO THE LORD

On the High Priest's forehead,
Carved on gold,
Hung these words:
"Holy to the Lord."

> Look at the forehead
> Of every man.
> Can you see the words?
> Can you make them out?
> "Holy to the Lord."

Are the letters much too faint?
You must see them with your heart—
"Holy to the Lord."

> Look in the mirror.
> Is your lipstick straight?
> Or, do you need a shave?
> Look again. Do you see the words?
> "Holy to the Lord."

With pride
The factory that made your car
Inscribed the maker's name
In letters that the world can see.
But God's mark is too faint:
"Holy to the Lord."

> A man is a thing of no value,
> Mass produced without the maker's name.
> Or can you see it?
> "Holy to the Lord."

Maybe God is not proud
Of His defective product.
Maybe He would just as soon forget
That each man once was meant to be
"Holy to the Lord."

> The pious Jew reminds God—and himself.
> On his forehead, in Tefillin,
> He can read the name of God.
> The Jew identifies himself:
> "Holy to the Lord."

Is that lipstick straight?
Or, do you need a shave?
Look again and see the writing
On your face:
"Holy to the Lord."

Exodus 39:30

FIRE AND WOOD

"The sons of Aaron shall put fire on the altar;
Then they shall arrange wood on the fire."

> First fire, then wood.
> But what is fire?
> It is not a substance.
> It is nothing independent
> Of the burning wood.
> How can there be fire without wood?

Sometimes I am weary, God.
Every bone aches.
Every muscle cries for rest.
The mind is dull.
The heart is sick.

> Sometimes the world crowds in
> And leaves no room for me.
> I want to lie down
> And shut the world out—or myself.

And yet there is a spark in me
That will not let me rest.

> Until this day
> I have always risen.
> Fire has overcome wood.

God, You are fire.
We are wood.
Wood without fire
Will not burn.
Fire without wood
Will not burn.

      Overcome me, God—
      All that is inert,
      All that lies dormant
      Waiting for the spark.

Let me act as if
All God's fire would go out
Without my poor wood.

      Sometimes I am weary.
      The mind is dull.
      The heart is sick.

Let me rise again
In flames of faith
To meet another day.

      Let me not decay.
      Let me burn.

Leviticus 1:7

THE FEAST AND THE LEAVINGS

"This is instruction for the Sacrifice of Well-Being that may be offered to the Lord . . . . What is left from the meat of the sacrifice shall be burned. . . . It becomes an abominable thing, and the person who eats it shall bear his guilt . . . ."

Our guilt.
We have eaten stale sacrificial flesh.
We have kept in cold storage
The remnants of ancient feasts,
And we have gnawed old bones.

Like the caterer's maid
After the wedding,
Making hash out of leavings.

Aleph, Bet, Gimel, Dalet,
Neat square letters competing on a page
With scribblings out of childish boredom—
Grandfather's sacrifice of joy,
Warmed over for our children
While we pursue well-being
Elsewhere.

Raising the scrolls in traditional ways,
Keeping time-honored moments of joy
Without the joy.
Motion without emotion.

　　It need not be so.
　　We can bring a new offering
　　Of gratitude and joy.

One offering alone is worthy—

　　With eyes open,
　　With ears listening,
　　With hearts eager,
　　Let us come before You, God,
　　Offering our joy.

You are our well-being,
As You were for our fathers,
If we will have it so.

　　Grandfather had the feast.
　　We have leavings,
　　Unless we make this sacrifice anew.

Leviticus 7:11, 17–18

LATE NEWS FLASH

" . . . Both were killed instantly. An investigation is in progress . . ."

And Aaron was silent.

"Here's further word on the spectacular tragedy that claimed the lives of two brothers . . ."

Aaron, the father, was silent.

" . . . Are determining whether the young men had been drinking. And now we switch you to our correspondent . . ."

His screams might have rent the world.
But he was silent.

" . . . Could not be reached for comment. Reporters who gathered outside were not admitted. We have to imagine the anguish of the parents who . . ."

* * *

God, You are merciful,
Withholding from us
Knowledge that would make us mad.

Aaron is always silent.
Even if he speaks
He does not know the words
To make us feel his pain.

We help him as we can.
But all the while we talk enough
To drown out Aaron's thoughts.

In time Aaron forgets.
Even Aaron finds time
For other problems.

> God, You do not let us see too deeply
> Into the heart of our fellow man.
> You make us forget the past;
> You do not let us see the future.

You insulate us just enough
From what we must not know
To let us go on living.

> Our problems are enough for us.
> You do not give us
> What we cannot bear.

Thank You for listening to cries
We cannot hear.

Leviticus 10:1–4

EMBRYOS

"When a woman conceives and gives birth . . . ."
Then most of the story is already told.

> From nothing to something,
> Nine months.
> One-celled animal
> To human being,
> Spanning in 280 days
> The history of life.

Our fate was determined in the womb.
Without our help or concern,
We grew then
Faster than ever after.

> As children we changed
> More slowly,
> But still we continued
> Man's adventure.

We inherited the thoughts and deeds
Of all who went before.
We became masters of the fate of
Kings and wise men, prophets, and rebels.

> History climaxed in us,
> In our forming persons.

Has it stopped?
Has our particular adventure
Run its course?

"When a woman conceives and gives birth . . . ."
Is that the beginning
Or the beginning of the end?
Do we begin to die, being born?
Is there but little growth left for us?

Forbid it, God.
Let us always be embryos,
Always changing, always growing,
Always adding to the story.

Do not let us rest.
Do not let us be
Our own graves.
Let us be Your partners
Now
In creating ourselves.

Leviticus 12:2

CONTAGION

"This is to be the law for the leper . . . ."
The leper masked his face
And cried, "Unclean! Unclean!"

> More fearful are diseases of the soul.
> For these there is no quarantine.

We roam free, spreading illness.
We wear no surgeons' masks
To keep our words from poisoning the air:

> "You know what she said to me *then* . . ."
> "He's a fine person, of course, but . . ."
> "You can't trust any of them."
> "You always do such stupid things."
> "Can't he do *anything* right!"

Discouragement is contagious.
Fear is infectious.
Our words breed illness.

> Hatred is a plague;
> Distrust, an epidemic.
> Our mouths spread disease.

The leper knew his infirmity,
And was ashamed.
We know, but shame is far from us.

> For our illness,
> God, do not blame us.
> Do not punish us for
> Our fears and our distress.

But help us
Not to spread these ills.

> Song is contagious, too.
> Cheer is infectious.
> Kindness multiplies.
> Love reaches out.

Help us nurture such germs
And spread them to the people that we meet.

> "You did that very well."
> "Let's stay here till we get it right."
> "Isn't this a beautiful day!"
> "I love my work!"
> "Let's help him."

For our illness,
God, do not blame us.
Do not punish us for
Our fears and our distress.

> But help us say things
> That will bring us health.

Leviticus 14:2 Midrash Rabbah

THE LAND IS HEAVING

Canaan and Rome are a memory—
Unbridled lust, spectacular death.

> "But you, you must keep My laws and My values
> And you must not commit any of these
>   depravities . . .
> So that the land does not vomit you up
> Because you defile it
> As it vomited up the people before you."

We do not need to read a list
Of the depravities.
Details are on the screens
Of local theatres:

> The pill, the thrill,
> The chill, the kill.

Diversion
From life without meaning.
Ultimate disbelief—
The suicide of joyless pleasure.

> Canaan had no vision of the future.
> Rome had only a past.
> What is our future?

The land is heaving now.
We can feel the nausea.

> God,
> We are in deepest need
> Of Your compassion.

71

Let us not be like
Bored prisoners,
Waiting only for death—
Seeking any way
To pass the useless time.

Tomorrow is demanding;
It calls for self-restraint.
The future is Your gift
To its believers.

Help us restore Your values.
Help us find faith in You
And in Your tomorrow.

The land is heaving now.
Help us believe in tomorrow.

Leviticus 18:26, 28

WITHOUT BEING VERY ODD

Fakeers fasting are holy men,
Contemplating the eternal.
    "You shall be holy:
      For I, the Lord your God,
      Am holy."
Celibates, mortifying flesh,
Are holy, too.
    "Do not steal,
    Or be false,
    Or lie one to another."
Holy is strange.
We dislike holy men.
The righteous and the pure
Are insufferable.
    "Do not go as a talebearer
    Among your poeple.
    Do not stand upon
    Your neighbor's blood."
We would not admit to being holy,
Even if it were true.
We are not religious.
    "Do not hate your brother
    In your thoughts,
    But tell your neighbor
    What you hold against him."
We are just average.
We do not pray much,
We have no inclination to pure thoughts.

"Do not take revenge
Or bear a grudge
Against those close to you.
Love your fellow man as yourself."
But we are as good as we can be—
Or want to be.

"Rise before the grey head.
Honor an old man.
Fear your God."
We might admit there is
Some room for improvement,
As long as you can guarantee
You will not call us holy.

"You shall maintain fair scales,
Fair weights,
Fair dry measure, fair liquid measure."

Maybe we would feel better
If we tried harder to keep these commandments,
At least these.
We can keep these without praying
Or being very odd.
Or can we?

"Be holy to Me
Because I, the Lord your God, am holy.
And I have separated you
From the other peoples
To be Mine."

To be Mine.

Leviticus 19

WHILE WE SLEEP

God, You give us the earth
And life.

> We do the work.
> We do the worrying.

We plow and sow,
Weed and hoe.
We have to get up early in the morning.
So much can go wrong.

> But while we sleep
> The crops spring up in secret.
> We never catch them growing.

One day—
Responding to the sunlight and the rain
As much as to our labors—
They are ripe.

> We do the work and the worrying,
> But while we sleep, they grow.
> While we rest, You do Your work.

And You ask nothing from us but a token:
"When you come to the land which I am giving you
And reap its harvest,
Then bring an Omer-full of the first of the harvest . . . .
To the Lord . . . ."

> From all Israel just an Omer,
> A small measure of grain,
> Just a reminder of what You do
> While we sleep.

Life is so hard!
There is no end to our problems.
We cannot work fast enough to keep ahead.

>But in the sleep of night
>Comes healing.
>The universe goes on without our help.
>We are refreshed by doing nothing,
>By trusting in Your presence.

Thank You for keeping watch in the night.
Thank You for being our partner.

>You do not ask much in return—
>An Omer, a sign of recognition.

That is the fee for the sunlight,
The fee for the rain,
The fee for watching while we sleep.

Leviticus 23: 10–13 Pesikta DeRav Kahana

MERELY TENANTS

"The land cannot be sold permanently,
Because the land belongs to Me,
And you are but residents on My sufferance."

We forget that nothing that we have is ours,
That we are merely tenants on the earth,
That everything is Yours.

You remind us.

Stalin bargained for whole cities.
His was the world's biggest empire.

All that remains to Stalin
Is the plot where he is buried—
And that is not secure.
Even graves do not endure.

We forget that our children are not ours.
You remind us.

If we fail to keep our trust,
If we are not the servants of posterity,
Our children become our doom.

We forget that our bodies are not ours,
Admiring our new clothes in the mirror,
Worrying about the turn of a cuff
Or the height of a skirt.

There are always new clothes.
But we shrink and fade.

> We forget that our minds are not ours
> When we gasp at all the things
> That man has done.

But we cannot control our thoughts.
We cannot escape our fears.
We are filled with envy and distrust,
Unless we put our trust in You.

> Only You are eternal.
> Nothing is ours
> Unless we know that we are Yours,
> Unless we do all that we do
> For You.

Leviticus 25:23

WE KEPT THE LAWS

"These are the laws and the statutes and the teachings
Which the Lord set between Himself and the people of
    Israel
On Mount Sinai through Moses."

    We kept the laws
    As well as men keep laws.
    We bent our will to Yours.

We heard Your word
And taught it to our young.
We kept the bargain.

    And blessings should have come to us.
    You promised to walk among us
    And be our God
    As we were Your people.

The laws are for You to keep,
Not only for us!

    But many who kept them are ashes.
    The saintly perished like the sinners.
    Each and every curse befell us,
    As if we had never done Your bidding.

You must keep the laws . . .
But we have not drawn conclusions . . .

    We still try to do Your will.
    We still believe there is reward for decency.
    We still believe that justice breeds justice.

We still feel shame at our sins,
Which are so small compared to Yours.

> We still allow ourselves to suffer
> Over suffering,
> As if we did not know
> It does not matter what happens to men.

Perhaps, looking at one of us—
A human being in tears at the death of a child
(Acting as if the child were somehow precious)—
You can believe in Yourself again
And do Your will.

> We are still Your people.
> We still care.
> Be our God.

Leviticus 26:46

THE FIRE WAITS

"They shall remove the ashes from the altar
And spread over it a crimson cloth . . .
And they shall put its poles in place . . .
When the camp prepares to travel. . . ."

> "And the fire
> Which had come down from heaven
> Would crouch beneath the cloth
> Like a lion
> During the time of travels. . . ."

That fire still burns.
It is not dead; it only waits.

> We are travelers
> Passing through this wilderness.

We are the cold altar
In which God's fire sleeps.

> The fire crouches like a lion,
> Waiting to enfold us in its flames
> If only we will stop.

Where is the fire of our love?
Smiles are frozen on our lips,
Polite, well meant, not meant,
Smiles of ice—

> Because we hurry on.
> We are travelers
> Passing through this wilderness.

Where is the fire of our longing
For that which is beyond us
Just out of grasp?

　　No time.
　　The fire waits.

It crouches like a lion
Waiting to burst forth
And seize us—
If only we will pause.

　　Lord who sent the fire!
　　Week by week You bid us rest.
　　Shabbat is home for the traveler.
　　Help us pause and lift the edge
　　Of the crimson cloth.

Numbers 4: 13—15 Rashi

WE MAY HEAR YOUR VOICE

"When Moses entered the Tent of Meeting to speak with God, he heard the voice speaking to him from above the cover on the Ark of Testimony—from between the two cherubim. Thus He spoke to *him.*"

> To Moses and to no one else.
> The people did not hear the voice.
> The priest did not hear it.
> Even the angels were deaf.

God, You speak at all times.
Your voice reaches the ends of the earth.
It is we who do not always hear.

> A baby cries for milk.
> In its wail we may detect a call for love—
> Your voice asking us to help You
> In forming this new personality.

A friend speaks.
He says yes, but means no.
He says, "I feel fine,"
While his heart aches.
He looks to us to understand.

> And Your voice joins his,
> Bidding us listen and understand
> And feel what our friend feels.

A boy shouts.
His words are wrong, offensive.
We do not want to listen.
But Your voice may be heard above his:
"It is not the words that count.
Do not listen only to the words.
Listen to the boy."

> We may hear Your voice
> On a silent summer's night
> When no one speaks
> And only crickets chirp
> And hearts beat.

We may hear Your voice
When we do something foolish, not reimbursing,
Because we would be ashamed
To do the prudent thing.

> The ear cannot sense these things,
> But sometimes we hear
> Sounds that do not come on waves of air.
> Your voice is everywhere.
> God, help us hear Your voice.

Numbers 7:89 Midrash Rabbah

BEHA·ALOTEKHA

ALSO ON DAYS OF JOY

"The Lord said to Moses: Have two silver trumpets
    made. . . .
And when you sound the alarm on the trumpets
You shall be remembered before the Lord your God,
And you shall be saved from your enemies.

"Also on your days of joy . . .
When you raise a blast on the trumpets . . .
They shall serve as reminder of you
Before your God."

Of all the ancient holy vessels
Lost, destroyed, and hidden,
Surely we need the trumpets now.

On them we should sound such alarms
That heaven would shake
And God would remember us.

Our cries do not reach.
Oh that we had the silver trumpets!

Somewhere they lie corroded and stained.

We always blew them in despair,
Sharp, anguished notes of fear;
And God remembered us.

But on our days of joy
We forgot.
We did not raise the blast
Of thankfulness and satisfaction.

Though joys came to us,
We did not draw the trumpets forth.

> One day the enemy came,
> And we trembled. We remembered—
> The trumpets, the silver trumpets!

We raised the trumpets to our lips.
We sucked in breath
In order to prolong metallic shrieks.

> But no sound came.
> No one still remembered how to blow the trumpets.

And God did not remember us.
One of the enemy, curious,
Picked up two blackened relics.
Idly, he threw them on the ruins of the city.
The rubble of the ages covered them.

> No trumpets have we,
> Nor can our cries reach heaven.
> We must train our voice with shouts of joy
> And thanksgiving.

Numbers 10:1–10

CREATOR OF GIANTS

"So they spread evil report of the land: . . .
'All the people we saw in it are men of gigantic size . . .
And we seemed to ourselves like grasshoppers,
And so we seemed to them.'

    "And the Lord said to Moses,
    'How long will this people despise Me?
    And how long will they have no faith in Me,
    In spite of all the wonders I have done among them?' "

Mankind,
Self-made grasshoppers,
Waiting to be stepped on,
We feel ourselves shrinking,
We who once were giants.

    Our voices, which once roared,
    Have turned to senseless chirps.

We hop this way and that,
Remembering nothing
Except that we are small.

    How long will we cower,
    Waiting for some impersonal foot
    To crush us?

How long will we laugh at ourselves
And mock our own movements,
Seeing no reason even to hop,
Since it is all the same.

    God, how long?—
    Until we recognize Your wonders.

You are the creator of giants.
When we believe in You
We believe in man.
In You we find ourselves.

Faith turns grasshoppers to men.

It is time for the revolt
Of the grasshoppers,
For the end of chirping
And the resumption of speech;
For walking straight instead of hopping.

Those who despise You despise themselves,
Creator of mankind!
Those who believe in You trust themselves,
Creator of giants!

Numbers 13:32–33; 14:11

MUCH USED WOOD

Aaron's rod that blossomed and bore fruit,
Some say, was his from generations past;
And often had it yielded forth great wonders.

> And Aaron's rod it was that brought deliverance
> In later times to Israel's kings.
> It will be seen again some day,
> Held by the Messiah.

Great was Aaron to draw miracles
From much used ancient wood.

> Greater the Messiah
> Who can take a tired relic,
> Worn by the hands of all his fathers,
> And produce yet one more miracle.

We are tired of wonders,
Weary of escapes from death.

> This is an old world.
> Man is drunk with miracles,
> Staggering under pain and joy.
> What wonder has Messiah left for us?

We would rather a new world,
Unused, unabused by history,
Unburdened by events—

> A world where Moses never crossed the Sea,
> Nor had to;
> A world where David never cried to God,
> Nor had to;

A world which never heard of love,
Because it never knew of hate;
A world which never saw deliverance,
Because it never suffered slavery;
A world which never received God's consolation,
Because it never tasted death.

> We would want a world without a past,
> A world which never needed miracles.

But this is our world.
And does it hold some miracle yet unperformed?

> Can Messiah, old man—
> Eyes bleary with weeping—
> Do something new with this old relic?

Tired world,
Tired people,
Tired Messiah,
Handed down from generations past,
Too often the source of wonder—

> We must have one miracle left—
> The miracle that ends miracles.

Numbers 17:21 Midrash Rabbah

FRAGMENTS OF AN UNKNOWN BOOK

"Therefore it is written in the book *Wars of the Lord*:
'Vahev by storm and the brooks of Arnon,
And the slope of the brooks. . . . ' "

    Strange fragment of an unknown book,
    Mysterious words from the lost long ago.

How many books have been written
That we shall never read?
How many songs have been sung
That we shall never hear?

    Many more are the unspoken thoughts
    Of unknown men
    That we shall never think.

Man's memory preserves
Lofty thoughts that changed the world.

    Burned on our hearts are the mighty deeds of heroes.
    Seared in our souls are the songs of inspired poets.

But where are the songs of the lowly
And the deeds of common men?
Where is immortality for books
Whose parchment rotted in the soil?

    Shall we dream in vain
    If our dreams are never told?
    Who will remember us?

God, remember us!
Regard our deeds.
Hear our thoughts.
Remember our songs.

> Our simple pleasures,
> Our uninspired hopes,
> Our unsublime thoughts,
> Our small fears,
> Our chronic pains—
> God, remember them.

We whom history will not mention
Live in You.

> You alone hold all in memory.

When earth shall have ceased
And books be no more,
You will remain and remember—

> And what we do day by day
> Will remain and be remembered.

Numbers 21:14

BALAK

WE TOO ARE SORCERERS

"Balak . . ., who was king of Moab at the time,
Sent messengers to Bil'am . . .:
'A certain people has come out of Egypt . . .
Lay a curse on this people for me . . .
Perhaps then I can attack and drive them from the land—
For I know that whoever you bless is blessed,
And whoever you curse is cursed.' "

    Bil'am, wiseman from the East—
    His very words had awesome power.
    Nations could buy his blessings.
    Kings could commission his curses.

How many were slain by his tongue?
And how many by ours?

    For we too are sorcerers.
    Our words bring blessings and curses, like his.

Who forgets a father's encouragement
Or a mother's comforting words?

    Who forgets angry speech?
    Who does not swallow as poison
    Even unmeant curses?

Who does not crave his friends' good wishes?
Who does not long to hear them spoken?

    Even when we play our games
    We call upon givers of blessing
    Chanting, incanting ritual rhymes,
    Cheering us on to win.

And when we fight our wars
We must have letters from home:
"Our thoughts are with you."
"We believe in what you're fighting for."

> Minor Bil'ams sell their wares
> On greeting cards:
> "Get well very soon. We miss you."

At the end of life we remember words,
Words we spoke and words we heard,
Words we did not speak and words we did not hear:

> "I love you." "I miss you."
> "Be strong. You can do it!"
> "God be with you."
> Bil'am had no words mightier than these.

Numbers 22:4–6

ZEALOT

Pinhas, burning zealot,
Stands forever poised,
Spear in hand,
Heart pounding with anguish,
Fighting battles for the Lord.

> And we, lesser men, do not love him.
> He frightens us
> With his narrowed eyes,
> With his absolute knowledge
> Of the way we must go.

And yet we go.
We follow Pinhas or his kind
To glory or to death.
One Pinhas atones for
All our vacillations.

> And still he lives,
> Always apart,
> With unmixed passion for the Lord.

We are objects;
Pinhas is force.
We are the unremembered, the extras,
Fit for the crowd scenes.
We are the background
For the man who knows the way.

> But who is Pinhas now?
> And who is Zimri?
> Who is zealous for the Lord?
> And who, His enemy?

For Zimri burns with passion, too—
And Zimri lives,
The animal, the appetite, the destroyer,
The zealot for himself alone.

Who is Zimri?
Who is Pinhas?
Which one is the madman for the Lord?

Voices cry on every side,
The mingled cries of zealots,
All with anger in their hearts
And hope on their lips.
Whose voice shall we hear?

Guide our hearts, Lord!
Help us know
Who is Zimri,
Who is Pinhas.

Whose voice shall we heed?
Forgive us for being only followers;
And help us to be led by You.

Numbers 25

BUT NOT THE CHILDREN

"We have many interests here,"
Said the men of Reuben.
"This is good land for cattle—
And we have cattle.

> "This is good land for us,
> Better than the land
> God promised to our fathers.

"Moses, we shall be with our brothers in spirit.
We shall send our sons to fight.
We shall send a portion of our riches
For the people of Israel—
But do not make *us* cross the Jordan.

> "Let us build pens for our cattle here,
> And cities for our children."

Moses wept and shook with anger,
But he let the men of Reuben
Build outside of Canaan
For their cattle and their children.

> The cattle thrived on the fertile plateau,
> But not the children.
> A generation passed
> And there were those who feared
> The children would forget
> That they were part of Israel.

"This must not be," said the elders of Reuben
As they erected a great altar to the Lord,
Not for sacrifice and service—
For that is done in Israel alone—
But for memorial.

> "Someday," they explained to Joshua,
> "Your sons will say to ours,
> 'You have no share in the Lord, you men of Reuben.'
> And we shall point to this altar.
> It is not for sacrifice and service,
> But for memorial alone."

The wars continued, but there came a day
When the men of Reuben did not send their sons,
But stayed by their cattle pens.

> Generations came and went.
> We do not hear of Reuben much again.
> The cattle thrived, but not the children.

Numbers 32. Joshua 23. Judges 5:16

MASSE

YOU WILL REMEMBER THE PLACES

"These are the stages
By which the people of Israel in their multitudes
Made their journey from Egypt, led by Moses and Aaron.

    "Moses wrote down their places of departure,
    Stage by stage, by the word of the Lord."

By the word of the Lord Moses wrote them,
Recording each place in its order.

    So we know where we have been
    And what we did there.

For who of us remembers yesterday?
Though it be written in the lines of our faces,
Though it be echoed in our footsteps;
Who can recall it as it happened?

    What came first? What happened then?
    Where did we do that? Why did we do that?

The names of places rise up in no order—
Migdol and Marah,
Cordova and Cracow,
Tel-Aviv and Cleveland—
We have been in all of them.

    We have been in so many places—
    Homes and hospitals,
    Streets and markets,
    Battlefields and graveyards,
    Places of birth and marrying and dying,
    Places where we lived
    And places where we failed to live.

Our past is always with us.
We are what we have done
And where we have been.

> Help us, Lord,
> To go where You would lead us;
> And help us to do what You would have us do,
> So that some day
> When we ourselves shall not recall all the places,
> The places will be known because of us.

And You will remember the places.
Someday perhaps You will remind us,
As You reminded Moses.

> May our journey find favor in Your sight.
> Help us in our journey, Lord.

Numbers 33:1, 2

EVERY PATH TO ANYWHERE

The people of Israel cried out to Moses
To show them the way to the Land:
"There is no way without difficulty!"

> God, that is so!
> No way at all.
> Every path to anywhere
> Twists and turns.

You made us to be travelers
On steep and winding roads.

> So we value nothing easy.
> We love mountaintops.

Our heroes do not go the easy way,
But reach their goals weary.

> Glory to those
> Who believe the unbelievable,
> Who have unreasonable hopes,
> Unattainable desires.

Easy ways go nowhere.
What we have we do not value.
What eludes us is our desire.

> There is no way without difficulty!
> And so—the way to You.

We cannot reach out and touch You.
You do not come to us by day and shout,
"Here I am. Believe, because you see!"

> You do not come to us.
> We must go to find You.

We must give our hearts to You.
We must believe in You
When there is least reason to believe.

> We must obey You
> When least You seem to hear our cries.

The way to You is filled with pits and boulders.
God, show us the difficult way to You.

Deuteronomy 1:22 Rashi

ONE

"Hear, O Israel:
The Lord is our God; the Lord is one."

    One, not many.
    We must not worship any force but You—

Not Love, not Wealth, not Art,
Nor any Cause;
For these are gods that disappoint.

    Men worship mere aspects of their lives;
    And many is the man who outlives such gods
    And comes to call them ashes.
    But You are ours forever,
    Because You are one, not many.

Hear, O Israel:
The Lord is our God; the Lord is one.

    One, not two.
    Life's evil, like the good,
    Comes from You, and from no other god.

Our terrors, like our joys,
Come from You, who love us.

    We do not understand why we must suffer,
    But *You* do,
    Because You are one, not two.

Hear, O Israel:
The Lord is our God; the Lord is one.

    One, not none.
    All life's rich variety
    Does not spring forth by chance.

Nor are we toys of fate,
Born to die forgotten
By blind nature.

>What we do—all that we do—
>Has meaning forever.
>You give us that meaning
>Because You are one, not none.

One, all is one.
All starts and ends in You.

>Hear, O Israel:
>The Lord is our God; the Lord is one.
>Blessed be Your name forever!

Deuteronomy 6:4

IF WE FORGET

"Be careful not to forget the Lord your God . . .
Otherwise, when you have plenty to eat
And live in fine houses you have built
And have much silver and gold,
You will grow proud . . .

    "And you will think to yourself,
    'My own strength and my own energy
    Have afforded me this wealth.' "

We shall really think it.
We shall really believe
That our wealth is ours by right,
If we forget You, God.

    We shall think we are what we have—
    Our food, our houses, our gold—

And besides we shall be nothing,
If we forget You, God.

    And we shall look down on our brothers
    Who have no fine houses
    And wonder what mistake they made
    And pity them
    From the safety of our houses.

And when our possessions tire us,
We shall look for new diversions
To see what else we can create
Out of our own boundless energy.

    We shall even play at poverty,
    Mingling with the poor in fashionable rags
    Till we tire of that, too.

And if we lose our wealth,
What shall we be then?
What will be believe?

    Will we call life a fraud;
    And, man a joke?

Our food is poisoned.
Our houses scar the land.
Our gold buys us weapons of war.
This is our strength and our energy.

    When we can no longer believe in ourselves,
    God, help us believe in You,
    So that we can believe in ourselves.

Deuteronomy 8:11–18

MOTIONS AND EMOTIONS

"You shall rejoice on your festival. . . .
And you shall be altogether happy."

> Joy!
> The highest commandment
> And the hardest of all.

God, if we believed,
If we truly believed in Your presence,
How could we be unhappy?

> Yet, though we seek it,
> Happiness eludes us.

How can You *command* us to be happy?
And how shall we obey?

> You have shown us how.
> Though we cannot force emotions
> We can act *as if* with joy.

If we cannot be happy,
We can still smile.

> If we cannot feel thankful,
> We can still say words of praise.

If we cannot love our fellow man,
Still we can help him,
Because thus You command.

> If we cannot feel festive,
> We can still set the table,
> Light the candles,
> Pour the wine,
> Sing the songs.

If we smile, maybe others will smile back.
If we say words of thanksgiving,
Maybe we shall come to feel them.

> If we help our fellowman,
> Maybe we shall be warmed by our deeds.

If we celebrate the feast,
Perhaps festivity will come.

> And joy, joy unbounded,
> Joy complete, joy overflowing—
> Joy will come to us.

Help us to go through the motions
That will bring us the highest emotions.

Deuteronomy 16:14, 15

THE UNKNOWN DEAD

On a blustery cloud-heavy day
A sad procession winds
Down to a rocky valley.

> Priests and elders stand
> On the barren shore of a shallow stream
> To offer expiation,

For they have found an unknown dead man,
Murdered in their midst.

> They wash their hands
> In flowing water
> And cry out to God:

"Our hands have not shed this blood!
We did not see the deed!
God, forgive Your people.
Do not let this innocent blood
Stain Your people Israel!"

> But that was long ago.

When murderers multiplied
The rite fell into disuse.

> Today we do not cry,
> "Our hands have not shed this blood!"

Our elders would be always
Washing hands.

> There are not rivers in the world
> Nor are there tears
> To wash away the blood.

109

Our hands have shed this blood!
Our eyes did see
But looked aside.

    We are used
    To finding the unknown dead.

We read it in the papers.
We sigh. We turn the page
To see what else is new.

    Nothing else is new.
    When blood is cheap,
    What else can matter?

Deuteronomy 21:1−9 Sifre

FORGETTING

"If while harvesting your crops
You forget a sheaf in the field,
Do not go back to pick it up.
It shall be for the stranger, the orphan, the widow. . . ."

> Forget!
> But we cannot forget,
> We who let our riches be our worries!

Why can we not forget possessions?
Why can we not run free and scatter sheaves?

> God, help us leave behind
> The things that weigh us down.

If while harvesting our days
We forget a day of sorrow—
If such a day should fall from memory,
May we never return to think on it.

> Why can we not forget!
> Why must we hold so tight
> What we should leave behind us?

If while harvesting our tears
We forget how those we love
Have done us wrong—
If we forget a tear,
Then may we never bring it forth again
To cloud our eyes.

> But how shall we not remember
> All the worries that we hoard—

Our property,
Our sorrows,
Our grudges—

    How shall we forget them?

Let us be like that rich man
Who, though not forgetting what he owned,
Still purposefully left the sheaves behind—

    And having left them,
    Later found he did not know their number.
    They were gone.

Deuteronomy 24:19

MIRACULOUS GARMENTS

"Moses called to all Israel and said to them: . . .
'I have led you through the wilderness for forty years.
The clothes on your backs have not worn out,
Nor have the shoes on your feet become old.' "

 The clothes they wore stayed new for forty years!
 And the garments of the children grew with them!

But the clothes in their trunks became faded and old,
And the shoes in storage moldered.

 Nor was this the only miracle.
 All that they had grew with use:

The silver they gave away became a Sanctuary.
The silver they hoarded corroded.

 The books they studied were remembered and
  copied.
 The books on the shelves crumbled to dust.

The labors they did made them stronger.
The strength they saved diminished their strength.

 The time they used well gave them more time.
 The hours not used slipped away forever.

The knowledge they used brought them more knowledge.
The knowledge they neglected fled from memory.

 The love they displayed created more love.
 The love they withheld died.

And we are the same.
Miraculous garments belong to us all.

    If we wear them, they grow.
    If we store them, they perish.

This miracle is ours.
We have the power to perform it
Every day, any day.

    We can restore what the moths have gnawed
    By putting on—now—our miraculous clothes.

Deuteronomy 29: 1, 4 Midrash Rabbah

CHOOSE LIFE

"I call the sky and earth
As witnesses towards you this day
That I have set before you
Life and death, blessing and curse.
Choose life."

> When next the crescent moon
> Adorns that selfsame sky
> And lights that selfsame earth,
> We shall gather to renew our pledge to life.

Once each year we pause
In our race from the unknown to the unknown,
And we ask: What is life?

> What is it we must choose?
> What brings us blessing?
> Why have we so often failed to find it?

Choose life?
Not merely years.

> Tortoises live longer than we,
> And yet we would not be like them,
> Entombed in armor.

We have to live vulnerable,
Nerves exposed,
Our quick movements dashing us
Against the world, against each other,
Against ourselves.

>We must always scurry, always search.
>If only we knew our goal!

What must we do
So that our life may triumph over our death?

>"Love the Lord your God,
>Obey Him and cleave to Him;
>For He is your life."

God, help us turn to You.
You are eternal; we pass.
Help us to participate in Your eternity.
Help us trust in You. Help us obey You.

>Help us choose life.
>Help us choose You.

Deuteronomy 30: 19–20

VAYELEKH
(Shabbat Shuva—before Yom Kippur)

LIKE SELF-SUFFICIENT ADAM

"It is the Lord your God who walks with you.
He will not leave you alone nor stray from your side."

> What makes us come again—
> If only once each year—
> To seek You, God?

Why do we crowd together
As if hoping to find in each other
Some assurance that we do belong to You?

> Our thoughts so little turn to You
> At other times.
> We are at peace without You . . .
> Or so it seems.

Why can we not altogether free ourselves
And forget You?

> We are like self-sufficient Adam
> Roaming Eden by himself,
> Having all he wanted
> Except . . . he knew not what.

He wandered restlessly.
Something would not let him be.
Something would not stray from him—
A need, a longing, an incompleteness.

> He studied every passing creature,
> Searching, seeking,
> Though he tried to think of other things.

So we need You.
Though we do not know You,
We always feel Your unseen presence.

>You will not let us be.
>You hover at our side.
>We can never quite escape You.

We have sought substitutes.
We lose ourselves in work or play.
We take up Causes.
We have tried to fall in love with ourselves,
To no avail.

>We are restless still.
>We feel You, just out of reach.

We shall come again to seek You.
We cannot help it.

Deuteronomy 31:6. Genesis 2:20–23

WITHOUT HAVING WALKED
THE PROMISED LAND

"The Lord spoke to Moses: . . .
'Go up to these mountains of Avarim to Mount Nebo . . .
And behold the land of Canaan,
Which I am giving to the people of Israel . . .
And die on the mountain which you shall climb . . .

    " 'You shall see the land from afar,
    But you shall not go there. . . .' "

Once he had pleaded to see his journey's end
And walk with his people in the promised land.

    But it was not to be.
    And it was well.

A sorrowing people escorted their leader
To the mountain's slope.
At his signal they departed with averted eyes.

    He climbed the mountain of vision
    And let his gaze wander across the river.

In the valley that he saw below
Abraham had battled with mighty kings.
On a distant ridge was the road
That took Father Jacob into exile.

    The past was known.
    What would the future bring?

In his mind he saw sheep grazing on the distant hills,
Laughing girls drawing water at the fountain,
Happy young men seeking the word of the Lord
From prophets yet unborn.

It was well.
He would never see his dream fulfilled,
But neither would he see his dream defiled.

He would not see the altars of obscene Baal,
His worshipers writhing in abhorrent rites.
He would not live to have men forget him and his God.

Each of us, like Moses, will die
Without having seen all he would see,
Without having walked his promised land.
It is well.

Better a dream unfulfilled
Than a vision brought low.
Who would have a dream
That—on this earth—can be fulfilled?

God, give us nobler dreams than we can realize!

Deuteronomy 32:48–52

120

SPIRAL

Again we have reached the end of the story.
Again we have begun at the beginning.
The tale comes full circle once a year—
But it is not a circle, rather a spiral
Coming back upon itself ever higher.
Each year we understand something more.
Each year the Torah illumines
Parts of our life we never knew were there.
God, make us wiser year by year.
May we draw ever more strength from Your word.
Grant us the joy of this day of completion
And beginning.
May our faith spiral upward . . .

HOLY DAYS AND
SPECIAL SABBATHS

AS YOU REMEMBERED SARAH

"The Lord remembered Sarah as He had promised;
The Lord did for Sarah as He had spoken:

> "Sarah conceived and bore Abraham a son
> In his old age."

And then nothing was simple anymore.
It was easier to become a mother
Than to be one.

> It was easier to hope for the impossible
> Than to accept the challenge
> Of her dream fulfilled.

Her son grew,
Bringing more dreams,
More desires,
More pain.

> "Thank You, God, for my son.
> Now may I live to wean him . . .
> Thank You, God, for letting me wean him.
> Now help me raise him to be loyal . . .
> Thank You, God, for all that is good in my son.
> Now help me find him a wife . . ."

God, remember us
As You remembered Sarah,
Replacing old desires
With new hopes.

> Today we pray for life.
> Today we ask for health and prosperity.
> Give us these things.
> But do not give us quiet hearts.

For quiet begins in the grave,
The end of pain
And the end of hope.

> Keep our dreaming unfulfilled.
> Give us ever-new hopes
> And the strength for ever-new worries.

Remember us
As You remembered Sarah.

> Give us life
> And life's new problems.

Genesis 21:1−2

HEARTS BOUND WITH LOVE

God,
We cannot comprehend
What You asked of Abraham:

> "Take your son,
> Your only one, whom you love—
> Isaac. . . .
> And offer him up as a sacrifice."

We are the children of Abraham,
Believing what we cannot comprehend:

> We believe You require human sacrifice—
> Not of bodies bound with ropes,
> But of hearts bound with love.

We believe our sacrifice is dear to You,
That the gift of our hearts builds the world.

> We believe that what we say matters to You,
> That our words vanishing into the wind
> Echo forever.

We believe our deeds matter,
That in Your sight
Our daily trifles rival in importance
The awesome galaxies.

> We believe that what we do today—
> Baring our hearts before You,
> Seeking Your presence,
> Calling Your name—
> Is the reason You created us.

We believe You remember those two fragile forms:
Isaac's young body on the altar
And his father, bowed with years,
Who did not flinch before Your will.

We believe that the faith of those two mortals
Long ago, unobserved by other eyes than Yours,
Is the fabric of our lives.

Though imprisoned in our mortal frames,
We, like them, can do Your will—
Every day of our lives.

We believe You require human sacrifice—
Not of bodies bound with ropes,
But of hearts bound with love.

Genesis 22:2

FOREVER?

"This is a most holy Sabbath for you,
And you shall afflict yourselves.
It is a law forever."

> Forever?
> God, forever?

Then what have we achieved today?
What good is our fasting?
What good is our solemnity,
If we and our children must repeat it
Forever?

> Why do we have to repeat our prayers?
> Why must we always seek fresh atonement?

Everything seems to be changing.
God, is anything forever?

> Today we need not pray for health.
> We have wonder drugs and skilled surgeons.

We need not stare in wonder at the moon.
We can go there.

> We exorcise no devils anymore.
> We have drugs to change men's personalities.

We need not read old books
When new ideas sweep the earth.

> Why, then, do we have to do today
> What our fathers did?

Or have we not changed?
Are we still primitive people
Doing again and again
Things we know are evil?

       Must we always fight against ourselves?
       Is that battle never won?

"And you shall afflict yourselves.
It is a law forever."

       If we cannot win the battle,
       Help us, at least, not to lose it.
       It is better to struggle forever
       Than to die once.

Leviticus 16:31

YOM KIPPUR—AFTERNOON

GOD TO JONAH

"God changed His mind about the disaster
He had intended for Nineveh; and he did not do it.

"But Jonah was extremely upset and very angry.
He prayed to the Lord:
'Oh, Lord, is not this what I said when I was at home—
That is why I fled to Tarshish in anticipation—
Because I knew that You are a compassionate and
merciful God,
Slow to anger and full of love, reversing evil
sentences.
So, Lord, take away my life,
Because I would rather die than stay alive.'

"And God said:
'Are you good and angry?' "

* * *

Are you good and angry, Jonah,
That Nineveh has not gone up in flame?

But the city was worth saving
Even though its people are still just people.
They are not what they ought to be,
But they admit their evil.
They are trying.

Jonah, that is enough!
Why should you be more demanding than your God?

My business is to forgive.
Who made it your business to destroy?

Why do some of My best people
Want to see the world destroyed?
Why are history books full of
Zealots burning and killing—for a better world!

Jonah, those are people in Nineveh!
I love them.
Why do some prophets think they know more about
   running the world
Than I do?

Do not be impatient, Jonah.
Burning cities will not bring a better day,
Only death.
Those are people!
I love them. I made them.
I do not ask them to be perfect,
Just to try a little harder.

Jonah, Jonah, little man,
Stupid man,
I did not make the world
As a place for perfect cities.
I made it for men—just like you.
I want their love, not their death.

Jonah, are you good and angry?
I am sorry to disappoint you.
But those are people!

Jonah 3:10; 4:1—4

IMPERMANENT DWELLINGS

"When Israel went forth from Egypt,
The House of Jacob from a people of strange tongue,
Then Judah became His sanctuary,
Israel His dominion."

> For forty years our fathers wandered
> In the wilderness.
> They were Your sanctuary;
> You were their protection.

"The Lord is my strength and my song;
He has become my salvation.
The joyful song of salvation
Is in the tents of the righteous."

> Tents, huts, Sukkot, rude impermanent dwellings—
> The weakest of structures were the strongest of
> homes.
> In them You shaped our people's soul.
> In them we felt Your nearness.
> We build these huts anew each year
> To find again Your presence.

"It is better to take refuge in the Lord than to trust in
man;
It is better to take refuge in the Lord than to trust in
princes."

> Life is frail as a Sukkah;
> Man is insubstantial as a harvest hut.
> Exposed to the ravages of nature, man is
> impermanent.

Life is strong as a Sukkah.
Man is enduring as a harvest hut;
Often beaten down, he rises again.

"I shall not die, but live;
And I shall recount the works of the Lord.
The Lord has sorely chastened me,
But He has not given me over to death."

Faith in God is frail as a Sukkah.
It is prey to all life's evil
Even as the Sukkah is exposed to wind and rain.

Faith in You is strong as a Sukkah.
Amid all life's furies it rises again and again,
A fortress of hope and salvation.

"Redeemer, prosper Your people who seek You
In every season.
Raise up again the fallen Sukkah of David. . . .
Remember Your people assembled.
Shelter Your folk who raise their tent in Your protecting
    shadow."

On Sukkot we thank You for all Your blessings—
Home and hearth, food and clothing.
Above all we thank You for the faith that sustains us.
Spread over us always Your Sukkah of inner peace.

Hallel. Zulat "B'nai Afar Mee Manah"

THE END IS THE BEGINNING

The end is the beginning.
This is the last of the holyday season,
The end of celebration.
Now begins the humdrum.
God, help us live our everyday
In the spirit of this festive time;
And with joy and exaltation in the tasks
You have allotted us.

> The end is the beginning.
> This holyday completes the reading of the Torah.
> The parchment rolls to the end.
> We come to the bare wood of the "tree of life"
> That holds the sacred manuscript.
> It is finished.

And right away, without a pause,
We start again to study Israel's heritage:
The end is the beginning.

> Nature has its final show of glory:
> Apples, plums, and grapes.
> The leaves turn red—then brown:
> "For You, Lord,
> Make the wind to blow,
> And the rain to fall."

The end is the beginning.
The buds of spring's new leaves
Already nestle at bare bark.

The dead leaves of the forest are blankets
For the roots of living trees.
The cold rain that lashes us
Brings life again after death.

> Rain! We pray for rain—
> Rain for the land of Israel, rain for the dry land,
> Rain for the holy land—
> For blessing, for life, and for plenty.
> Rain is the end—and the beginning.

On this day we recall in love
Dear ones whom we see no more.
As we honor them today, we know
The end is the beginning.
For men and women whose memory is sacred
There is no end.

> Daily we hold dearer in memory
> Parents whose words we did not always heed;
> Brothers and sisters with whom we quarreled;
> Children with whom we exchanged harsh words,
> Though gladly we had died for them.
> Husbands and wives. . . .

They all live on in us.
Knowing them taught us what we know.
Losing them brought us life's unlearned lesson.
Remembering them has made us remember ourselves.

> Hold them close, Lord. They live in You.
> And teach us so to live that
> Our end will be our beginning.

WHY SHOULD I SAY THANK YOU?

Why should I say thank You, God?
Sometimes I do not feel so very good.

> There are days when nothing goes right,
> Whole weeks I wish I could erase.

There has been much sickness here,
And some of my friends have problems worse than mine.

> I am frightened by the trouble in our cities.
> It is not safe these days to walk the streets.

I met someone who knows a friend
That lost a boy at war.

> I like to think the world is getting better,
> But sometimes it is very hard to think that.

Still, once in a while I go out in the country,
Where it is quiet, and I can think.

> Even when bare of leaves, a tree is a glory
> When I stop to look at it.

There has been much good in my life.
Sometimes I glimpse the pattern of the passing generations.

> Sometimes, in my worst moments, I have tried harder
> And made up for my own lacks.

I know no answers to war and hate.
I wish I could always control myself, never mind the world.

> But I keep trying. And sometimes I pause to look at
> myself.
> I am alive. Tomorrow may be good or bad. But now I
> am alive.

I can hope that You, who made the trees,
Will help me conquer myself.

> Why should I say thank You, God?
> Because then I feel much better.

When I say thank You—I mean: God, You made a
beautiful world,
And You made it for me—and I will try a little harder to
be worthy.

IN DARKNESS CANDLES

Lord, You create day and night,
Rolling away light before darkness,
Darkness before light.

> Thank You for the darkness.
> Without it we could not appreciate the light.
> By the darkness we can measure blessing—

Health by sickness,
Laughter by tears,
Riches by poverty,
Freedom by oppression.

> In the darkness of the night
> The Maccabees lit a flame
> Which still illuminates our lives.
> Thank You for the challenge that they met.

In centuries of night
Men rose at midnight and lit flames.
And by those slender lights,
From torn and tear-soaked prayerbooks,
They pleaded for Your mercy
And asked an end to exile's night.

> Thank You for the answer to their prayers.
> Thank You for restoring Israel's light.

But still night reigns
In all the world.

> Thank You for unfinished tasks.
> In the darkness
> Teach us to light candles.

Teach us to light candles,
Even as we did tonight
In memory of ancient light after darkness.

A candle is small.
Not far from where it brightly flames
The darkness closes in.

But candles light other candles,
And light draws strength from light.
Each night of life let us add candles:

The candle of hope.

The candle of faith.

The candle of brave deeds.

The candle of freedom . . .

Thank You for the darkness.
Thank You for the light.

Maariv

DO NOT COUNT THEM

Joe died
And Jack died.
John lost a leg.

>Not a bad day—
>Only three casualties.
>The enemy must have lost a hundred.
>Not a bad day.

* * *

Only eight per cent of the students failed.
That is better than last year
By three-tenths of one per cent.

>Only eight per cent is a good record.
>Other schools envy us.

* * *

Moses had to know how many were his people,
How great was his army, how strong were his forces.

>It was a sin to count the men.
>But he had to know.

"The Lord spoke to Moses:
'When you take the sum of the Israelites
As they are enrolled,
Each shall pay the Lord a ransom for his life . . .
So that there will be no plague upon them
Through being numbered . . .
Half a shekel.' "

139

Moses counted shekels,
But not men.
Men must not be counted.
Men are not a commodity.

Joe is Joe.
Jack is Jack.
John is John.
Add them together.
Do not say "three men."
Say "Joe and Jack and John."
Do not do sums with them.
That is the plague.

Look at the eight per cent who failed.
They have faces.
Do not count them.
That is the plague.

Exodus 30:11–13

SOMEDAY WHEN WE LAUGH

BLESSED ARE YOU, LORD OUR GOD, KING OF THE
UNIVERSE, FOR SANCTIFYING US WITH YOUR COM-
MANDMENTS AND FOR COMMANDING US TO READ
THE MEGILLAH.

> Once again we read of Haman's schemes,
> And once again we do not laugh.

We have studied our history,
But still have been condemned,
Over and over, to relive it.

> Now we have read the story
> Once too often.
> It is written in the blood
> Of Jewish children,
> Inscribed in the smoke of Auschwitz.

BLESSED ARE YOU, LORD OUR GOD, KING OF THE
UNIVERSE, FOR MAKING MIRACLES FOR OUR
FATHERS LONG AGO AT THIS SEASON.

> Miracles have come once more.
> There is a land where Haman cannot rise again
> And cannot come to say:
> "There is a certain people,
> Scattered and dispersed . . .
> Whose laws are different
> From every other people. . . ."

There is a land
Where no indifferent king
Can summon us to die.

Thank You for miracles of long ago.
Thank You for helping us make new miracles
For which we bless You anew.

Someday when we laugh at Haman's antics
In a carnival, watching him duck pies,
We shall say:
Yes, that was long ago and far away,
And never will it come to pass again.

That day is still not here.
We cannot laugh at Haman yet.
But there is a land
Where miracles are being fashioned now.

This is the time of anguish.
This is the time of joy.

This is the time of birth pangs.
And we, of all the generations that have passed,
Can hope to laugh again at Purim time.
We thank You for the privilege of being alive now.

BLESSED ARE YOU, LORD OUR GOD, KING OF THE
UNIVERSE, FOR KEEPING US ALIVE AND WELL
AND ENABLING *US* TO REACH THIS HAPPY TIME.

Blessings before reading the Megillah of Esther

WATER OF PURIFICATION

"He that touches a dead body . . . shall be unclean. . . .
And if a man becomes unclean and does not undergo
purification, then that person is cut off from the congregation, having defiled the Lord's sanctuary. If the water of
purification is not sprinkled on him, he remains unclean."

>Pesah is coming.
>The Lord's feast is near.
>In the spring of the year
>Cleanse yourselves.

The dead defile—
Dead men and
Dead dreams and
Dead thoughts and
Dead deeds.

>The spring rain sweeps away
>The last dead leaves of autumn.

The dead cannot praise God,
But we can,
By refusing to die with the dead.

>Winter was long.
>We looked out at gathering shadows
>And thought of last spring.

We saw ourselves laughing
With loved ones who can laugh no more.
We caught ourselves dreaming
Of things that cannot be.

And we denied God.
Our thoughts defiled us,
Dead thoughts
That would have killed us, too.

Tears are waters of purification,
Releasing the debris of hearts,
Sweeping away the dull glaze
Of sleepless eyes.

       Prayers are purification.
       We prayed, not believing,
       Not knowing what to pray, what to say,
       What to hope.

Spring rain, sweep away dead leaves.
Cut raw gashes in fertile earth,
And let tender grass spring up again.

       Come, water of purification.
       Cleanse us of death's flirtation.

There are other summers.
Pesah is coming.
The Lord's feast is near.
In the spring of the year
Let us be cleansed.

Number 19:11, 20

DEADLINES

"This month for you is the first of months. . . ."

> Countdown for Pesah.

"On the 10th of this month each man shall take a lamb per family. . . ."

> Arrange for your Seder now.

"You shall watch over it until the 14th of the month. . . ."

> The time is near.

"And all the congregation of the Israelite community shall slaughter it toward evening."

> Deadline after deadline,
> A procession of times,
> Year after year,
> Generation after generation.

There is a time for men,
A schedule of events in life.

> Children are born to young women.
> There is a deadline.

Children learn best when young.
There is a time.

> Crawl, toddle, walk, read.
> There is an age.

Want ads and posters agree:
18 to 25 years of age,
25 to 45 years of age,
Till 65, till 70.
Join us now, not later.

> And the earth changes its colors
> From white to green to brown
> Only so many times
> Before it is over.

There is always a season coming,
Always a time that is near.
Let us meet our deadlines.

> Let us do the things we have to do
> While it is still time to do them.

Let us say the things we have to say
While there is still time to say them.

Exodus 12:2–6

BEFORE THE DESTRUCTION

"The utterance of the Lord's word to Israel by Malachi: . . . .
I will send you Elijah the prophet
Before the great and terrible Day of the Lord;

>"And he shall make the hearts of parents responsive
>   to children,
>And the hearts of children to their parents,
>So that I shall not have to strike the earth
>With utter destruction."

* * *

The lights flash in spasms.
Bodies quiver in prophetic frenzy.
Drums and guitars surge in prophetic fury:

>WE ARE ON THE EVE OF DESTRUCTION!

Once at Pesah time
We had flowers and warm breezes,
Families coming together,
Parents and children,
Warmth and affection.

>This Pesah
>There are children who will not be coming home,
>Nor celebrating at their parents' feast.

And their empty places,
Like the untouched goblet on the table,
Will be waiting for Elijah.

>Every Pesah we recall Elijah.
>God, send him now,
>On the eve of destruction.

Make our hearts responsive
On the eve of destruction.

> We did not take it seriously—
> We taught the prophets' words
> To our young ones—
> They chanted to perfection,
> Understanding not a word.

They did not see the prophets' fire
In our eyes.
They did not feel their passion
In our deeds.
They did not believe we believed.

> We did not understand the words we made them
>   learn.
> Did You really mean You wanted our devotion—
> That You wanted us to do
> What You spoke through Your prophets?

Pardon us.
We did not understand.

Malachi 1:1; 3:23—24

WE CELEBRATE THE FUTURE

We do not celebrate the past,
Nor raise our cups to miracles of old.

> We shed no tears for Pharoah's slaves,
> Nor are we moved by memory
> Of Pharoah's chariots sinking in the sea.

We do not sing of them.
God, we do not praise You
Because our fathers were redeemed.

> We think of ourselves
> When we speak of ancient times
> And recall the miracles of long ago.

We think of new Pharoahs
In business suits.

> Our thanks are wishes.
> Our gratitude is hope.
> God, repeat Your miracles for us!

We celebrate the future.
We raise our cups to miracles to come:

> "No one will hurt or destroy
> On all my holy mountain,
> For the earth will be full of knowledge of the Lord
> As the sea is full of water."

Our bondage is like that of those two Hebrew slaves
That Moses saw fighting each other.

> Brother fought brother
> Because of the anguish of Pharoah's tyranny.
> Or was it the reverse?
> Do Pharoahs flourish
> Because brother fights his brother?

We celebrate the future
When we shall be free from spite and envy,
When we shall not wound each other,
When we shall not climb upward
Over the prostrate bodies of our brothers,
When—because we know the Lord—
A Pharoah cannot come to be.

> We celebrate the Pesah of the future
> When we ourselves shall not hurt and destroy.

Isaiah 11:9. Exodus 2:13

150

DAY OF SMALL THINGS

"Who has despised the day of small things?"

> The prophet spoke to discouraged men.
> The parade had passed.
> The great deeds had been done.
> Now the details.

We have seen glory too.
The world watched
As Israel was reborn in flame.

> Success is sweet wine.
> What follows is a tasteless brew.

The enemies are still about.
The brave die unapplauded.
The nations resume their indifference.

> Another Day of Independence.
> Joy is mingled with sorrow and fear.
> Tomorrow is another work day,
> Not so inspiring.

It is the same here.
It is easy to cheer when flags are raised.
It is easy to step forward when emotion wells.

> But we have our daily tasks.
> They fill us with accustomed weariness.
> Where do we go from here?

"Who has despised the day of small things?"

The small things:
In Israel it means
Devotion to one's job,
Putting up with bad service,
Paying exorbitant taxes,
Worrying about one's son,
Trying to win an education.

The small things:
Here it means
Even greater support of our brothers,
Renewed devotion to the synagogue and the home—
The fortresses of our spirit.
It means shrugging off discouragement.
It means bearing the load that others leave.

Events that stir us do not come often.
Daily cares are with us always.
Lord, give us the strength for small things.

Zechariah 4:10

ORPAH

Orpah turned her head and walked away,
Softly, sadly.
She looked back one more time
As if drawn against her will,
And then went home.

>She had been kind.
>Bound by widows' grief,
>She had stayed by the side of the other two
>For many days.
>She had wept with them.
>She had vowed to share their destiny.

But Naomi was right—
Orpah could not always follow her,
Nor should she always mourn.
She was young.
Among her own people she would find another love.

>The years passed.
>Often she wondered what had been the fate
>Of Ruth and Naomi.
>"Have you been in Bethlehem?
>And do you know a widow Naomi?
>Tell me . . . how does she look?"

Thank God for Ruth!
For Ruth had stayed with Naomi
And brought back color to her cheeks
And the twinkle to her eyes.

      Ruth was Naomi's match for wit and skill.
      She had made things right.
      She too was married now, had a child.
      Her husband was not young, but a good man
      And grateful for Ruth's kindness.

Orpah was relieved.
It was well with Naomi.
It was well with Ruth.
It was well, too, with Orpah.
Everyone, after all, had done what was best.

      And yet Orpah could not help but think
      That once she had turned her head and walked away.
      She had done what she should—
      Everyone would agree, everyone—
      But she had turned her head and walked away.

Book of Ruth

154